3-D THRILLERS!

DINOSAURS

HEATHER AMERY

Capella

Millions and millions of years before any people lived on Earth, the world belonged to the dinosaurs! These amazing creatures first appeared about 228 million years ago (**mya** for short). Though their name means 'terrible lizard', these prehistoric reptiles were not actually lizards, and many were not particularly terrible (unless you were a plant!). Some were as small as a chicken; others were longer than three buses in a row. From the knee-high to the sky-high, dinosaurs ruled the Earth for about 160 million years. Humans have only been around for about 1.5 million years, so we have a lot of catching up to do!

DINOSAUR DAYS

Dinosaurs lived during the Mesozoic Era, which began 245 mya and ended 65 mya. Each of three periods in the Mesozoic Era had its own cool creatures. The Triassic Period (248–206 mya) gave us the earliest dinosaurs, like *Herrerasaurus* (eh-ray-rah-SORE-us), as well as the first small mammals. The Jurassic Period (206–142 mya) produced plant-eaters like *Stegosaurus* (steg-oh-SORE-us) and meat-eaters like *Allosaurus* (al-oh-SORE-us). And the Cretaceous Period (142–65 mya) was the time of *Iguanadon* (ig-WHA-noh-don) and *Deinonychus* (die-NON-i-kus) – and, sadly, the end of the line for the dinosaurs.

EMPTY NESTERS

Like most reptiles, dinosaurs laid and hatched from eggs. For many years, palaeontologists (scientists who study prehistoric life) thought that dinosaurs were pretty relaxed parents, to put it mildly: in their tough neighbourhood, maybe self-preservation was considered a higher priority than taking care of the children! But some fossils now indicate that certain dinosaurs may have been very protective of their young, like one Cretaceous plant-eater who apparently guarded its babies and brought them food. Palaeontologists named this dinosaur *Maiasaura* (my-ah-SORE-ah), or 'good mother lizard'. Thanks, mum!

CAN YOU DIG IT

When most dinosaurs died, their bodies just rotted away and nothing remained of them. But if a dinosaur died and the conditions were right, the bones would gradually become petrified (turned to stone). By examining these ancient remains, called fossils, palaeontologists can learn what a dinosaur looked like, how it moved, and what – or who! – it ate for supper. Fossils of prehistoric animals and plants are found all over the world – maybe even in your own back garden!

Scientists believe that there are hundreds of dinosaur species yet to be found. So start digging – the next news- breaking discovery may be yours!

arnivorous dinosaurs, the most fearsome, wouldn't have won any popularity contests. Some, like the recently discovered **Giganotosaurus** (JI-gah-NO-tuh-SORE-us), were humongous, but there were also mini meat-munchers like **Compsognathus** (komp-soh-NAY-thus), which was no bigger than a modern chicken. But they all had the same favourite meal — MEAT — and the tools to get it. When their dagger-like, flesh-ripping teeth fell or wore out, new ones grew in to take their place. No dentures for these dudes!

Eaters

FOOD FIGHTS

While some herbivorous (plant-eating) dinosaurs may have been gentle, they didn't necessarily give up without a struggle. In Mongolia's Gobi Desert, the bones of a meat-eating *Velociraptor* (vel-O-si-RAP-tor, meaning 'speedy robber') and the bones of a plant-eating *Protoceratops* (pro-toe-SER-a-tops) were found together, indicating a fight to the finish – for both of them. So much for fast food!

ARMED AND DANGEROUS

At under 11 metres long, *Allosaurus* was the top predator of the Jurassic Period. It had a powerful tail, three strong claws on each hand, and a mouthful of teeth with jagged edges perfect for tearing and chewing flesh. You wouldn't hear this diner complain that his meat was too tough!

The great meat-eater Megalosaurus (MEG-ah-loh-SORE-us), or 'great reptile', was the first dinosaur ever to be named. When its leg bone was unearthed, people first thought they had discovered the remains of a giant man.

The biggest creatures that have ever walked the Earth were the herbivorous (plant-eating) dinosaurs. The neck alone of the **Mamenchisaurus (mah-MEN-chee-SORE-us)** measured 12 metres long — the length of a bus. Another long-neck, **Seismosaurus (SIZE-moh-sore-us)**, may have measured nearly 40 metres. That's the length of two bowling alley lanes! The plant-eaters went looking for food, not trouble, so other dinosaurs had little to fear from them. But a meat-eater that provoked or attacked them might get more than it bargained for. The three facial horns and neck shield of **Triceratops (try-SER-a-tops)** made it hard for a carnivore to get in a good chomp. And **Ankylosaurus (an-KIE-loh-SORE-us)** had a rock-hard ball at the end of its tail to club any attackers. Talk about mean cuisine!

VEGETARIAN VENGEANCE

Imagine long-necked reptiles the height of six men standing on each other's shoulders and as heavy as a dozen elephants! *Brachiosaurus* (brak-ee-oh-SORE-us) was way too massive to move fast. But it had a thick and powerful tail, great for whacking Jurassic attackers like *Allosaurus* and *Ceratosaurus* (seh-rat-oh-SORE-us). And while its thick, tree-like limbs weren't built for speed, *Brachiosaurus* might have been able to rear back on its hind legs and crash its front ones down on its enemy. Take that!

TOUGH LOVE

The plant-eating *Pachycephalosaurus* (PAK-ee-SEF-a-loh-SORE-us) was a real bonehead! The solid dome on the top of its skull was 25 centimetres thick. Some scientists believe that during the mating season, rival males would fight for females by charging at each other headfirst. Those built-in crash helmets certainly came in handy.

ENTLE GiaNTS?

WEAPONS OR WEATHERPROOFING?

The strange-looking *Stegosaurus* has long puzzled palaeontologists.
Most now agree that its triangular plates formed a row down its back
and served as a sort of prehistoric furnace *and* air-conditioner.
Stegosaurus may have turned its plates towards the sun to soak in rays
to warm its body, while a breeze through the plates would cool it down.
Scientists used to think that the plates discouraged predators from
snacking on *Stegosaurus*, but further study has revealed that they
weren't really too sturdy. Fortunately, the one-metre-long, spear-like
spikes on its tail would have been excellent weapons.

Poor *Stegosaurus* has another
claim to fame besides its weird
appearance: Its walnut-sized
brain was smaller than
any other dinosaur's.

The
polished
pebbles found among
some plant-eating dinosaur remains
suggest that before they gulped
down their leafy lunches, some
plant-eaters may have
swallowed stones to help
grind up the food in
their stomachs,
like some
birds do
today.

Tyrannosaurus

W hen you hear the word 'dinosaur', what comes to mind first? Bet you said T. rex! **Tyrannosaurus rex (tie-RAN-oh-SORE-us REX)**, whose name means 'king of the tyrant lizards', was definitely one of the biggest, hungriest and fiercest meat-eating dinosaurs. Standing 6 metres tall and 13 metres long, it

S: The Ex-Rex?

It would have taken about 290 teachers a year to keep a *Tyrannosaurus Rex* fed!

ALL THE BETTER TO EAT YOU WITH

Tyrannosaurus rex was certainly a bigmouth! With a head as long as a refrigerator, it could have opened its jaws wide enough to swallow a man in one gulp. Curved, jagged teeth, longer than a human hand, could puncture its prey's organs before tearing it apart. *T. rex*'s teeth were made for ripping, not chewing, so it had to swallow each mouthful whole. What dreadful table manners!

SUPER-REX

In 1990, one of the largest and most complete *Tyrannosaurus* skeletons ever unearthed was found in South Dakota, USA. Named 'Sue', after its discoverer, this fossilized dinosaur was a real tough customer. A number of its bones had been broken but had rehealed over time. The broken bones were probably a result of fierce battles with other *T. rex*.

THE RIGHTFUL KING

Giganotosaurus, whose name means 'giant lizard of the south', was discovered in Argentina in 1993. When this dinosaur's skull and thigh bone measured bigger than Sue's, it became clear that *Tyrannosaurus* was *rex* no more! How long will *Giganotosaurus* be number 1? Its reign could end at any time, since new types of dinosaurs are being found every year. But until then – Long Live the King!

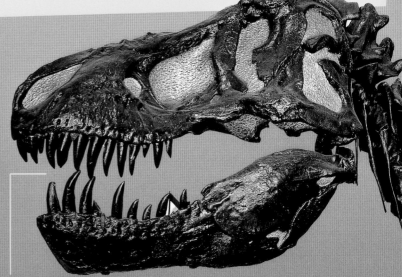

While dinosaurs roamed the Earth, equally awesome beasts ruled the seas. Many of these oceanic monsters evolved from land reptiles and adapted to life in the water. But though some looked pretty fishy, they were still reptiles, and had to come to the water's surface to breathe between dives, like whales and dolphins do. The prehistoric sea monsters came in all shapes and sizes. Some had long necks and flippers, while others had long jaws filled with razor-sharp teeth. One of the biggest, **Kronosaurus (KRON-oh-SORE-us)**, with its 2.5 metre head, feasted on prehistoric squids, sharks — and its fellow seafaring reptiles!

Beautifully preserved fossils suggest that *Ichthyosaurs* didn't lay eggs but gave birth to their little ones live in the water.

GONE FISHIN'

Ichthyosaurs (IKH-thee-oh-sores), like this 15-metre-long *Shonisaurus* (shon-ee-SORE-us), were the super swimmers of the prehistoric seas. They looked and lived a lot like modern-day dolphins – but they were much, *much* bigger. With their sleek bodies, back fins, and strong tails, the *Ichthyosaurs* zipped through the water as fast as 40 kmph. When their big eyes spotted a tasty meal, their long, tooth-lined jaws would open and *snap!* Fish du jour!

MONSTERS

MONSTER OR MYTH?

Sea monster sightings have been reported all over the world. The most famous of these creatures is Scotland's 'Nessie', the so-called Loch Ness Monster. Descriptions of Nessie – and a photo that turned out to be a fake – made it sound like a plesiosaur. Few people believe there are any such monsters today ... but never say never!

DOWN IN THE DEPTHS

With their skinny necks and roly-poly bodies, *Plesiosaurs* (PLE-see-oh-sores) may have looked awkward, but thanks to paddle-like flippers that let them twist and turn, they were able to swim at high speeds to catch food with their sharp teeth. To help themselves sink, they sometimes swallowed rocks to act as ballast. Now there's an appetizer that would fill anyone up!

In prehistoric times, reptiles not only ruled the Earth and seas but also filled the skies. The **Pterosaurs** (Teh-ruh-SORES), flying reptiles with wings made of skin, fed on creatures from both land and sea. Some were as tiny as a sparrow, but others had a wingspan the size of a small aeroplane's — along with knife-sharp teeth. Look out below!

AIR-VOLUTION

Rhamphorynchus (RAM-foh-RING-khus), one of the early pterosaurs, had spiky teeth, great for spearing fish. It also had a long, kite-like tail that may have helped it steer through the skies. Later flying reptiles like *Quetzalcoatlus* looked quite different, with much shorter tails but longer necks.

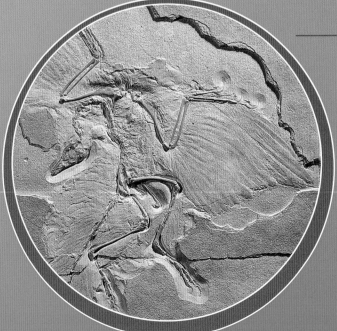

FINALLY ... FEATHERS!

Archeopteryx (ark-ee-OP-ter-iks), which means 'ancient wing', is the first flying reptile known to have had feathery wings. But don't let the feathers fool you – this was no ordinary bird. Its fossils reveal a skeleton of a reptile with dinosaur-like teeth and claws on its wings, which it may have used to climb trees. Some scientists think it may have been more of a glider than a flier – okay at catching a breeze, but lousy at take-offs!

he dinosaurs (and their airborne and seafaring relatives) ruled for 165 million years. But 65 mya, they all disappeared. What happened? Did something kill them all at once, or did they gradually become extinct over a year … a decade … a millennium? Did one catastrophic event wipe out prehistoric life, or did a combination of factors cause this disappearing act? There are several theories that try to answer these questions. But until someone invents a time machine to take us back to the dinosaur days, we may never know exactly what happened to these amazing beasts.

VIOLENT VOLCANOES

One theory blames the dinosaurs' disappearance on huge volcanoes in what is now India. These volcanoes erupted late in the Cretaceous Period, and may have spewed so much lava, volcanic ash and poisonous gas into the air that the dinosaurs couldn't survive the climate change. Just another example of the dangers of passive smoking.

LIGHTS OUT

At the end of the Cretaceous Period, a massive meteorite – more than 10 kilometres wide – may have crashed down on Earth. Many scientists think that the huge clouds of dust from this collision blocked out the sun for weeks or maybe even months. Plenty of small animals (such as mammals, birds and insects) survived this big bang. However, without sunlight most plant life died. The dinosaurs would have starved to death or frozen in the freezing conditions caused by there being no sun.

BABY, IT'S COLD OUTSIDE

A less dramatic explanation of extinction is that Earth's climate changed gradually and the creatures that lived there changed with it. Once warm and tropical, our planet's weather got drier and cooler, which was fine for some creatures but devastating for dinosaurs, who couldn't handle the big chill.

Believe it or not, here are some of the wackier suggestions about what happened to the dinosaurs:

They ate all the plants and starved to death.

Rat-sized mammals ate all their eggs.

Space aliens carried them away. (Hmm... maybe there are *Velociraptors* on Venus and a *Maiasaura* on Mars!)

What do you think?

This edition published in 2008 by Arcturus Publishing Limited
26/27 Bickels Yard, 151–153 Bermondsey Street,
London SE1 3HA

Copyright © 2001 Arcturus Publishing Limited

Editors: Anne Fennell and Paula Field
Designers: Susi Martin and Leah Kalotay
Author: Heather Amery
Illustrator (glasses): Ian Thompson

Picture Credits:

Copyright © Natural History Museum (London): Front & back cover;
Page 1; page 2 bottom right; pages 3 - 10; pages 14 - 16.

Copyright ©: Ardea: Page 2 top left; page 11 top right ; page 12 page 13
bottom right.

Copyright © Discovery Communications Inc: Page 11 bottom;
page 13 top right.

3-D images produced by Pinsharp

Printed in China

ISBN: 978-1-84193-006-0